Knitting

Project: _____

Start Date: _____ Finish: _____

Measurements: _____

Materials	Quantity
_____	_____
_____	_____
_____	_____

Needles	Embellishments
_____	_____
_____	_____

Gauge

_____sts per _____ inch(es)

_____rows per _____ inch(es)

Other Tools

_____

_____

Knitting Journal

Project: _____

Start Date: _____ Finish: _____

Measurements: _____

Materials	Quantity
_____	_____
_____	_____
_____	_____

Needles	Embellishments
_____	_____
_____	_____

Gauge	Other Tools
____sts per ____ inch(es)	_____
____rows per ____ inch(es)	_____

Knitting Journal

Project: _____

Start Date: _____ Finish: _____

Measurements: _____

Materials   Quantity

_____   _____

_____   _____

_____   _____

Needles   Embellishments

_____   _____

_____   _____

Gauge   Other Tools

_____ sts per _____ inch(es)   _____

_____ rows per _____ inch(es)   _____

Knitting Journal

Project: _____

Start Date: _____ Finish: _____

Measurements: _____

Materials   Quantity

_____   _____

_____   _____

_____   _____

Needles   Embellishments

_____   _____

_____   _____

Gauge   Other Tools

_____ sts per _____ inch(es)   _____

_____ rows per _____ inch(es)   _____

Knitting Journal

Project: _____

Start Date: _____ Finish: _____

Measurements: _____

Materials   Quantity

_____   _____

_____   _____

_____   _____

Needles   Embellishments

_____   _____

_____   _____

Gauge   Other Tools

_____ sts per _____ inch(es)   _____

_____ rows per _____ inch(es)   _____

Knitting Journal

Project: _____

Start Date: _____ Finish: _____

Measurements: _____

Materials   Quantity

_____   _____

_____   _____

_____   _____

Needles   Embellishments

_____   _____

_____   _____

Gauge   Other Tools

____sts per ____ inch(es)   _____

____rows per ____ inch(es)   _____

Knitting Journal

Project: _____

Start Date: _____ Finish: _____

Measurements: _____

Materials

_____

_____

_____

Quantity

_____

_____

_____

Needles

_____

_____

Embellishments

_____

_____

Gauge

_____ sts per _____ inch(es)

_____ rows per _____ inch(es)

Other Tools

_____

_____

Knitting Journal

Project: _____

Start Date: _____ Finish: _____

Measurements: _____

Materials	Quantity
_____	_____
_____	_____
_____	_____

Needles	Embellishments
_____	_____
_____	_____

Gauge	Other Tools
_____ sts per _____ inch(es)	_____
_____ rows per _____ inch(es)	_____

Knitting Journal

Project: _____

Start Date: _____ Finish: _____

Measurements: _____

Materials   Quantity

_____   _____

_____   _____

_____   _____

Needles   Embellishments

_____   _____

_____   _____

Gauge   Other Tools

_____ sts per _____ inch(es)   _____

_____ rows per _____ inch(es)   _____

Knitting Journal

Project: _____

Start Date: _____ Finish: _____

Measurements: _____

Materials	Quantity
_____	_____
_____	_____
_____	_____

Needles	Embellishments
_____	_____
_____	_____

Gauge	Other Tools
_____ sts per _____ inch(es)	_____
_____ rows per _____ inch(es)	_____

Knitting Journal

Project: _____

Start Date: _____ Finish: _____

Measurements: _____

Materials	Quantity
_____	_____
_____	_____
_____	_____

Needles	Embellishments
_____	_____
_____	_____

Gauge	Other Tools
_____ sts per _____ inch(es)	_____
_____ rows per _____ inch(es)	_____

Knitting Journal

Project: _____

Start Date: _____ Finish: _____

Measurements: _____

Materials	Quantity
_____	_____
_____	_____
_____	_____

Needles	Embellishments
_____	_____
_____	_____

Gauge	Other Tools
_____ sts per _____ inch(es)	_____
_____ rows per _____ inch(es)	_____

Knitting Journal

Project: _____

Start Date: _____ Finish: _____

Measurements: _____

Materials	Quantity
_____	_____
_____	_____
_____	_____

Needles	Embellishments
_____	_____
_____	_____

Gauge	Other Tools
_____ sts per _____ inch(es)	_____
_____ rows per _____ inch(es)	_____

Knitting Journal

Project: _____

Start Date: _____ Finish: _____

Measurements: _____

Materials	Quantity
_____	_____
_____	_____
_____	_____

Needles	Embellishments
_____	_____
_____	_____

Gauge	Other Tools
_____ sts per _____ inch(es)	_____
_____ rows per _____ inch(es)	_____

Knitting Journal

Project: _____

Start Date: _____ Finish: _____

Measurements: _____

      Materials   Quantity

_____   _____

_____   _____

_____   _____

      Needles   Embellishments

_____   _____

_____   _____

      Gauge   Other Tools

_____ sts per _____ inch(es)   _____

_____ rows per _____ inch(es)   _____

Knitting Journal

Project: _____

Start Date: _____ Finish: _____

Measurements: _____

Materials   Quantity

_____   _____

_____   _____

_____   _____

Needles   Embellishments

_____   _____

_____   _____

Gauge   Other Tools

_____ sts per _____ inch(es)   _____

_____ rows per _____ inch(es)   _____

Knitting Journal

Project: _____

Start Date: _____ Finish: _____

Measurements: _____

Materials	Quantity
_____	_____
_____	_____
_____	_____

Needles	Embellishments
_____	_____
_____	_____

Gauge	Other Tools
_____ sts per _____ inch(es)	_____
_____ rows per _____ inch(es)	_____

Knitting Journal

Project: _____

Start Date: _____ Finish: _____

Measurements: _____

Materials	Quantity
_____	_____
_____	_____
_____	_____

Needles	Embellishments
_____	_____
_____	_____

Gauge	Other Tools
_____ sts per _____ inch(es)	_____
_____ rows per _____ inch(es)	_____

Knitting Journal

Project: _____

Start Date: _____ Finish: _____

Measurements: _____

Materials	Quantity
_____	_____
_____	_____
_____	_____

Needles	Embellishments
_____	_____
_____	_____

Gauge	Other Tools
_____ sts per _____ inch(es)	_____
_____ rows per _____ inch(es)	_____

Knitting Journal

Project: _____

Start Date: _____ Finish: _____

Measurements: _____

Materials	Quantity
_____	_____
_____	_____
_____	_____

Needles	Embellishments
_____	_____
_____	_____

Gauge	Other Tools
_____sts per _____ inch(es)	_____
_____rows per _____ inch(es)	_____

Knitting Journal

Project: _____

Start Date: _____ Finish: _____

Measurements: _____

Materials   Quantity

_____   _____

_____   _____

_____   _____

Needles   Embellishments

_____   _____

_____   _____

Gauge   Other Tools

_____ sts per _____ inch(es)   _____

_____ rows per _____ inch(es)   _____

Knitting Journal

Project: _____

Start Date:_____ Finish: _____

Measurements: _____

Materials	Quantity
_____	_____
_____	_____
_____	_____

Needles	Embellishments
_____	_____
_____	_____

Gauge	Other Tools
_____sts per _____ inch(es)	_____
_____rows per _____ inch(es)	_____

Knitting Journal

Project: _____

Start Date: _____ Finish: _____

Measurements: _____

Materials	Quantity
_____	_____
_____	_____
_____	_____

Needles	Embellishments
_____	_____
_____	_____

Gauge	Other Tools
_____ sts per _____ inch(es)	_____
_____ rows per _____ inch(es)	_____

Knitting Journal

Project: _____

Start Date:_____ Finish: _____

Measurements: _____

Materials	Quantity
_____	_____
_____	_____
_____	_____

Needles	Embellishments
_____	_____
_____	_____

Gauge	Other Tools
____sts per ____ inch(es)	_____
____rows per ____ inch(es)	_____

Knitting Journal

Project: _____

Start Date: _____ Finish: _____

Measurements: _____

Materials	Quantity
_____	_____
_____	_____
_____	_____

Needles	Embellishments
_____	_____
_____	_____

Gauge	Other Tools
____sts per ____ inch(es)	_____
____rows per ____ inch(es)	_____

Knitting Journal

Project: _____

Start Date: _____ Finish: _____

Measurements: _____

Materials   Quantity

_____   _____

_____   _____

_____   _____

Needles   Embellishments

_____   _____

_____   _____

Gauge   Other Tools

____ sts per ____ inch(es)   _____

____ rows per ____ inch(es)   _____

Knitting Journal

Project: _____

Start Date: _____ Finish: _____

Measurements: _____

Materials   Quantity

_____   _____

_____   _____

_____   _____

Needles   Embellishments

_____   _____

_____   _____

Gauge   Other Tools

_____sts per _____ inch(es)   _____

_____rows per _____ inch(es)   _____

Knitting Journal

Project: _____

Start Date: _____ Finish: _____

Measurements: _____

Materials	Quantity
_____	_____
_____	_____
_____	_____

Needles	Embellishments
_____	_____
_____	_____

Gauge	Other Tools
_____ sts per _____ inch(es)	_____
_____ rows per _____ inch(es)	_____

Knitting Journal

Project: _____

Start Date: _____ Finish: _____

Measurements: _____

Materials	Quantity
_____	_____
_____	_____
_____	_____

Needles	Embellishments
_____	_____
_____	_____

Gauge

_____sts per _____ inch(es)

_____rows per _____ inch(es)

Other Tools

_____

_____

Knitting Journal

Project: _____

Start Date: _____ Finish: _____

Measurements: _____

Materials	Quantity
_____	_____
_____	_____
_____	_____

Needles	Embellishments
_____	_____
_____	_____

Gauge	Other Tools
_____sts per _____ inch(es)	_____
_____rows per _____ inch(es)	_____

Knitting Journal

Project: _____

Start Date: _____ Finish: _____

Measurements: _____

Materials	Quantity
_____	_____
_____	_____
_____	_____

Needles	Embellishments
_____	_____
_____	_____

Gauge

_____ sts per _____ inch(es)

_____ rows per _____ inch(es)

Other Tools

_____

_____

Knitting Journal

Project: _____

Start Date: _____ Finish: _____

Measurements: _____

Materials	Quantity
_____	_____
_____	_____
_____	_____

Needles	Embellishments
_____	_____
_____	_____

Gauge	Other Tools
_____ sts per _____ inch(es)	_____
_____ rows per _____ inch(es)	_____

Knitting Journal

Project: _____

Start Date: _____ Finish: _____

Measurements: _____

Materials   Quantity

_____   _____

_____   _____

_____   _____

Needles   Embellishments

_____   _____

_____   _____

Gauge   Other Tools

_____ sts per _____ inch(es)   _____

_____ rows per _____ inch(es)   _____

Knitting Journal

Project: _____

Start Date: _____ Finish: _____

Measurements: _____

Materials	Quantity
_____	_____
_____	_____
_____	_____

Needles	Embellishments
_____	_____
_____	_____

Gauge	Other Tools
_____ sts per _____ inch(es)	_____
_____ rows per _____ inch(es)	_____

Knitting Journal

Project: _____

Start Date: _____ Finish: _____

Measurements: _____

Materials	Quantity
_____	_____
_____	_____
_____	_____

Needles	Embellishments
_____	_____
_____	_____

Gauge	Other Tools
____sts per ____ inch(es)	_____
____rows per ____ inch(es)	_____

Knitting Journal

Project: _____

Start Date: _____ Finish: _____

Measurements: _____

Materials   Quantity

_____   _____

_____   _____

_____   _____

Needles   Embellishments

_____   _____

_____   _____

Gauge   Other Tools

_____ sts per _____ inch(es)   _____

_____ rows per _____ inch(es)   _____

Knitting Journal

Project: _____

Start Date: _____ Finish: _____

Measurements: _____

Materials	Quantity
_____	_____
_____	_____
_____	_____

Needles	Embellishments
_____	_____
_____	_____

Gauge	Other Tools
_____sts per _____ inch(es)	_____
_____rows per _____ inch(es)	_____

Knitting Journal

Project: _____

Start Date: _____ Finish: _____

Measurements: _____

Materials	Quantity
_____	_____
_____	_____
_____	_____

Needles	Embellishments
_____	_____
_____	_____

Gauge	Other Tools
____ sts per ____ inch(es)	_____
____ rows per ____ inch(es)	_____

Knitting Journal

Project: _____

Start Date: _____ Finish: _____

Measurements: _____

Materials	Quantity
_____	_____
_____	_____
_____	_____

Needles	Embellishments
_____	_____
_____	_____

Gauge	Other Tools
_____ sts per _____ inch(es)	_____
_____ rows per _____ inch(es)	_____

Knitting Journal

Project: _____

Start Date: _____ Finish: _____

Measurements: _____

Materials	Quantity
_____	_____
_____	_____
_____	_____

Needles	Embellishments
_____	_____
_____	_____

Gauge	Other Tools
_____ sts per _____ inch(es)	_____
_____ rows per _____ inch(es)	_____

Knitting Journal

Project: _____

Start Date: _____ Finish: _____

Measurements: _____

Materials   Quantity

_____   _____

_____   _____

_____   _____

Needles   Embellishments

_____   _____

_____   _____

Gauge   Other Tools

_____ sts per _____ inch(es)   _____

_____ rows per _____ inch(es)   _____

Knitting Journal

Project: _____

Start Date: _____ Finish: _____

Measurements: _____

Materials	Quantity
_____	_____
_____	_____
_____	_____

Needles	Embellishments
_____	_____
_____	_____

Gauge

_____ sts per _____ inch(es)

_____ rows per _____ inch(es)

Other Tools

_____

_____

Knitting Journal

Project: _____

Start Date: _____ Finish: _____

Measurements: _____

Materials	Quantity
_____	_____
_____	_____
_____	_____

Needles	Embellishments
_____	_____
_____	_____

Gauge	Other Tools
_____ sts per _____ inch(es)	_____
_____ rows per _____ inch(es)	_____

Knitting Journal

Project: _____

Start Date: _____ Finish: _____

Measurements: _____

Materials   Quantity

_____   _____

_____   _____

_____   _____

Needles   Embellishments

_____   _____

_____   _____

Gauge   Other Tools

_____ sts per _____ inch(es)   _____

_____ rows per _____ inch(es)   _____

Knitting Journal

Project: _____

Start Date: _____ Finish: _____

Measurements: _____

Materials	Quantity
_____	_____
_____	_____
_____	_____

Needles	Embellishments
_____	_____
_____	_____

Gauge	Other Tools
_____ sts per _____ inch(es)	_____
_____ rows per _____ inch(es)	_____

Knitting Journal

Project: _____

Start Date: _____ Finish: _____

Measurements: _____

Materials	Quantity
_____	_____
_____	_____
_____	_____

Needles	Embellishments
_____	_____
_____	_____

Gauge	Other Tools
_____ sts per _____ inch(es)	_____
_____ rows per _____ inch(es)	_____

Knitting Journal

Project: _____

Start Date: _____ Finish: _____

Measurements: _____

Materials	Quantity
_____	_____
_____	_____
_____	_____

Needles	Embellishments
_____	_____
_____	_____

Gauge	Other Tools
____sts per ____ inch(es)	_____
____rows per ____ inch(es)	_____

Knitting Journal

Project: _____

Start Date: _____ Finish: _____

Measurements: _____

Materials	Quantity
_____	_____
_____	_____
_____	_____

Needles	Embellishments
_____	_____
_____	_____

Gauge	Other Tools
_____ sts per _____ inch(es)	_____
_____ rows per _____ inch(es)	_____

Knitting Journal

Project: _____

Start Date: _____ Finish: _____

Measurements: _____

Materials	Quantity
_____	_____
_____	_____
_____	_____

Needles	Embellishments
_____	_____
_____	_____

Gauge	Other Tools
_____ sts per _____ inch(es)	_____
_____ rows per _____ inch(es)	_____

Knitting Journal

Project: _____

Start Date: _____ Finish: _____

Measurements: _____

Materials   Quantity

_____   _____

_____   _____

_____   _____

Needles   Embellishments

_____   _____

_____   _____

Gauge   Other Tools

_____ sts per _____ inch(es)   _____

_____ rows per _____ inch(es)   _____

Knitting Journal

Project: _____

Start Date: _____ Finish: _____

Measurements: _____

Materials	Quantity
_____	_____
_____	_____
_____	_____

Needles	Embellishments
_____	_____
_____	_____

Gauge	Other Tools
_____ sts per _____ inch(es)	_____
_____ rows per _____ inch(es)	_____

Knitting Journal

Project: _____

Start Date: _____ Finish: _____

Measurements: _____

Materials	Quantity
_____	_____
_____	_____
_____	_____

Needles	Embellishments
_____	_____
_____	_____

Gauge	Other Tools
____ sts per ____ inch(es)	_____
____ rows per ____ inch(es)	_____

Knitting Journal

Project: _____

Start Date: _____ Finish: _____

Measurements: _____

Materials	Quantity
_____	_____
_____	_____
_____	_____

Needles	Embellishments
_____	_____
_____	_____

Gauge	Other Tools
_____ sts per _____ inch(es)	_____
_____ rows per _____ inch(es)	_____

Knitting Journal

Project: _____

Start Date: _____ Finish: _____

Measurements: _____

Materials	Quantity
_____	_____
_____	_____
_____	_____

Needles	Embellishments
_____	_____
_____	_____

Gauge	Other Tools
_____ sts per _____ inch(es)	_____
_____ rows per _____ inch(es)	_____

Knitting Journal

Project: _____

Start Date: _____ Finish: _____

Measurements: _____

Materials	Quantity
_____	_____
_____	_____
_____	_____

Needles	Embellishments
_____	_____
_____	_____

Gauge	Other Tools
_____ sts per _____ inch(es)	_____
_____ rows per _____ inch(es)	_____

Knitting Journal

Project: _____

Start Date: _____ Finish: _____

Measurements: _____

Materials	Quantity
_____	_____
_____	_____
_____	_____

Needles	Embellishments
_____	_____
_____	_____

Gauge	Other Tools
_____sts per _____ inch(es)	_____
_____rows per _____ inch(es)	_____

Knitting Journal

Project: _____

Start Date: _____ Finish: _____

Measurements: _____

Materials	Quantity
_____	_____
_____	_____
_____	_____

Needles	Embellishments
_____	_____
_____	_____

Gauge	Other Tools
_____ sts per _____ inch(es)	_____
_____ rows per _____ inch(es)	_____

Knitting Journal

Project: _____

Start Date:_____ Finish: _____

Measurements: _____

Materials	Quantity
_____	_____
_____	_____
_____	_____

Needles	Embellishments
_____	_____
_____	_____

Gauge	Other Tools
____sts per ____ inch(es)	_____
____rows per ____ inch(es)	_____

Knitting Journal

Project: _____

Start Date: _____ Finish: _____

Measurements: _____

Materials	Quantity
_____	_____
_____	_____
_____	_____

Needles	Embellishments
_____	_____
_____	_____

Gauge	Other Tools
_____ sts per _____ inch(es)	_____
_____ rows per _____ inch(es)	_____

Knitting Journal

Project: _____

Start Date: _____ Finish: _____

Measurements: _____

Materials	Quantity
_____	_____
_____	_____
_____	_____

Needles	Embellishments
_____	_____
_____	_____

Gauge	Other Tools
____sts per ____ inch(es)	_____
____rows per ____ inch(es)	_____

Knitting Journal

Project: _____

Start Date: _____ Finish: _____

Measurements: _____

Materials	Quantity
_____	_____
_____	_____
_____	_____

Needles	Embellishments
_____	_____
_____	_____

Gauge	Other Tools
_____ sts per _____ inch(es)	_____
_____ rows per _____ inch(es)	_____

Knitting Journal

Project: _____

Start Date: _____ Finish: _____

Measurements: _____

Materials	Quantity
_____	_____
_____	_____
_____	_____

Needles	Embellishments
_____	_____
_____	_____

Gauge   Other Tools

_____ sts per _____ inch(es)   _____

_____ rows per _____ inch(es)   _____

Knitting Journal

Project: _____

Start Date: _____ Finish: _____

Measurements: _____

Materials   Quantity

_____   _____

_____   _____

_____   _____

Needles   Embellishments

_____   _____

_____   _____

Gauge   Other Tools

_____sts per _____ inch(es)   _____

_____rows per _____ inch(es)   _____

Knitting Journal

Project: _____

Start Date: _____ Finish: _____

Measurements: _____

Materials	Quantity
_____	_____
_____	_____
_____	_____

Needles	Embellishments
_____	_____
_____	_____

Gauge	Other Tools
____ sts per ____ inch(es)	_____
____ rows per ____ inch(es)	_____

Knitting Journal

Project: _____

Start Date: _____ Finish: _____

Measurements: _____

Materials	Quantity
_____	_____
_____	_____
_____	_____

Needles	Embellishments
_____	_____
_____	_____

Gauge	Other Tools
____sts per ____ inch(es)	_____
____rows per ____ inch(es)	_____

Knitting Journal

Project: _____

Start Date: _____ Finish: _____

Measurements: _____

Materials   Quantity

_____   _____

_____   _____

_____   _____

Needles   Embellishments

_____   _____

_____   _____

Gauge   Other Tools

_____ sts per _____ inch(es)   _____

_____ rows per _____ inch(es)   _____

Knitting Journal

Project: _____

Start Date: _____ Finish: _____

Measurements: _____

Materials	Quantity
_____	_____
_____	_____
_____	_____

Needles	Embellishments
_____	_____
_____	_____

Gauge	Other Tools
_____ sts per _____ inch(es)	_____
_____ rows per _____ inch(es)	_____

Knitting Journal

Project: _____

Start Date: _____ Finish: _____

Measurements: _____

Materials	Quantity
_____	_____
_____	_____
_____	_____

Needles	Embellishments
_____	_____
_____	_____

Gauge	Other Tools
_____ sts per _____ inch(es)	_____
_____ rows per _____ inch(es)	_____

Knitting Journal

Project: _____

Start Date: _____ Finish: _____

Measurements: _____

Materials

_____

_____

_____

Quantity

_____

_____

_____

Needles

_____

_____

Embellishments

_____

_____

Gauge

_____sts per _____ inch(es)

_____rows per _____ inch(es)

Other Tools

_____

_____

Knitting Journal

Project: _____

Start Date: _____ Finish: _____

Measurements: _____

Materials   Quantity

_____   _____

_____   _____

_____   _____

Needles   Embellishments

_____   _____

_____   _____

Gauge   Other Tools

____ sts per ____ inch(es)   _____

____ rows per ____ inch(es) _____

Knitting Journal

Project: _____

Start Date: _____ Finish: _____

Measurements: _____

Materials	Quantity
_____	_____
_____	_____
_____	_____

Needles	Embellishments
_____	_____
_____	_____

Gauge	Other Tools
_____sts per _____ inch(es)	_____
_____rows per _____ inch(es)	_____

Knitting Journal

Project: _____

Start Date: _____ Finish: _____

Measurements: _____

Materials   Quantity

_____   _____

_____   _____

_____   _____

Needles   Embellishments

_____   _____

_____   _____

Gauge   Other Tools

_____ sts per _____ inch(es)   _____

_____ rows per _____ inch(es)   _____

Knitting Journal

Project: _____

Start Date: _____ Finish: _____

Measurements: _____

Materials	Quantity
_____	_____
_____	_____
_____	_____

Needles	Embellishments
_____	_____
_____	_____

Gauge	Other Tools
_____ sts per _____ inch(es)	_____
_____ rows per _____ inch(es)	_____

Knitting Journal

Project: _____

Start Date: _____ Finish: _____

Measurements: _____

Materials	Quantity
_____	_____
_____	_____
_____	_____

Needles	Embellishments
_____	_____
_____	_____

Gauge

_____ sts per _____ inch(es)

_____ rows per _____ inch(es)

Other Tools

_____

_____

Knitting Journal

Project: _____

Start Date: _____ Finish: _____

Measurements: _____

Materials	Quantity
_____	_____
_____	_____
_____	_____

Needles	Embellishments
_____	_____
_____	_____

Gauge	Other Tools
_____ sts per _____ inch(es)	_____
_____ rows per _____ inch(es)	_____

Knitting Journal

Project: _____

Start Date: _____ Finish: _____

Measurements: _____

Materials	Quantity
_____	_____
_____	_____
_____	_____

Needles	Embellishments
_____	_____
_____	_____

Gauge	Other Tools
_____ sts per _____ inch(es)	_____
_____ rows per _____ inch(es)	_____

Knitting Journal

Project: _____

Start Date: _____ Finish: _____

Measurements: _____

Materials	Quantity
_____	_____
_____	_____
_____	_____

Needles	Embellishments
_____	_____
_____	_____

Gauge	Other Tools
_____sts per _____ inch(es)	_____
_____rows per _____ inch(es)	_____

Knitting Journal

Project: _____

Start Date: _____ Finish: _____

Measurements: _____

Materials	Quantity
_____	_____
_____	_____
_____	_____

Needles	Embellishments
_____	_____
_____	_____

Gauge	Other Tools
_____ sts per _____ inch(es)	_____
_____ rows per _____ inch(es)	_____

Knitting Journal

Project: _____

Start Date: _____ Finish: _____

Measurements: _____

Materials	Quantity
_____	_____
_____	_____
_____	_____

Needles	Embellishments
_____	_____
_____	_____

Gauge	Other Tools
_____ sts per _____ inch(es)	_____
_____ rows per _____ inch(es)	_____

Knitting Journal

Project: _____

Start Date: _____ Finish: _____

Measurements: _____

Materials   Quantity

_____   _____

_____   _____

_____   _____

Needles   Embellishments

_____   _____

_____   _____

Gauge   Other Tools

_____ sts per _____ inch(es)   _____

_____ rows per _____ inch(es)   _____

Knitting Journal

Project: _____

Start Date: _____ Finish: _____

Measurements: _____

Materials	Quantity
_____	_____
_____	_____
_____	_____

Needles	Embellishments
_____	_____
_____	_____

Gauge	Other Tools
____sts per ____ inch(es)	_____
____rows per ____ inch(es)	_____

Knitting Journal

Project: _____

Start Date: _____ Finish: _____

Measurements: _____

Materials   Quantity

_____   _____

_____   _____

_____   _____

Needles   Embellishments

_____   _____

_____   _____

Gauge   Other Tools

_____ sts per _____ inch(es)   _____

_____ rows per _____ inch(es)   _____

Knitting Journal

Project: _____

Start Date: _____ Finish: _____

Measurements: _____

Materials	Quantity
_____	_____
_____	_____
_____	_____

Needles	Embellishments
_____	_____
_____	_____

Gauge

_____ sts per _____ inch(es)

_____ rows per _____ inch(es)

Other Tools

_____

_____

Knitting Journal

Project: _____

Start Date: _____ Finish: _____

Measurements: _____

Materials	Quantity
_____	_____
_____	_____
_____	_____

Needles	Embellishments
_____	_____
_____	_____

Gauge	Other Tools
_____ sts per _____ inch(es)	_____
_____ rows per _____ inch(es)	_____

Knitting Journal

Project: _____

Start Date: _____ Finish: _____

Measurements: _____

Materials	Quantity
_____	_____
_____	_____
_____	_____

Needles	Embellishments
_____	_____
_____	_____

Gauge	Other Tools
____ sts per ____ inch(es)	_____
____ rows per ____ inch(es)	_____

Knitting Journal

Project: _____

Start Date: _____ Finish: _____

Measurements: _____

Materials	Quantity
_____	_____
_____	_____
_____	_____

Needles	Embellishments
_____	_____
_____	_____

Gauge	Other Tools
_____ sts per _____ inch(es)	_____
_____ rows per _____ inch(es)	_____

Knitting Journal

Project: _____

Start Date: _____ Finish: _____

Measurements: _____

Materials   Quantity

_____   _____

_____   _____

_____   _____

Needles   Embellishments

_____   _____

_____   _____

Gauge   Other Tools

____ sts per ____ inch(es)   _____

____ rows per ____ inch(es)   _____

Knitting Journal

Project: _____

Start Date:_____ Finish: _____

Measurements: _____

Materials	Quantity
_____	_____
_____	_____
_____	_____

Needles	Embellishments
_____	_____
_____	_____

Gauge	Other Tools
_____sts per _____ inch(es)	_____
_____rows per _____ inch(es)	_____

Knitting Journal

Project: _____

Start Date: _____ Finish: _____

Measurements: _____

Materials	Quantity
_____	_____
_____	_____
_____	_____

Needles	Embellishments
_____	_____
_____	_____

Gauge	Other Tools
_____ sts per _____ inch(es)	_____
_____ rows per _____ inch(es)	_____

Knitting Journal

Project: _____

Start Date: _____ Finish: _____

Measurements: _____

Materials	Quantity
_____	_____
_____	_____
_____	_____

Needles	Embellishments
_____	_____
_____	_____

Gauge	Other Tools
_____ sts per _____ inch(es)	_____
_____ rows per _____ inch(es)	_____

Knitting Journal

Project: _____

Start Date:_____ Finish: _____

Measurements: _____

Materials   Quantity

_____   _____

_____   _____

_____   _____

Needles   Embellishments

_____   _____

_____   _____

Gauge   Other Tools

____sts per ____ inch(es)   _____

____rows per ____ inch(es)   _____

Knitting Journal

Project: _____

Start Date: _____ Finish: _____

Measurements: _____

Materials	Quantity
_____	_____
_____	_____
_____	_____

Needles	Embellishments
_____	_____
_____	_____

Gauge	Other Tools
_____ sts per _____ inch(es)	_____
_____ rows per _____ inch(es)	_____

Knitting Journal

Project: _____

Start Date: _____ Finish: _____

Measurements: _____

Materials	Quantity
_____	_____
_____	_____
_____	_____

Needles	Embellishments
_____	_____
_____	_____

Gauge	Other Tools
_____ sts per _____ inch(es)	_____
_____ rows per _____ inch(es)	_____

Knitting Journal

Project: _____

Start Date: _____ Finish: _____

Measurements: _____

Materials	Quantity
_____	_____
_____	_____
_____	_____

Needles	Embellishments
_____	_____
_____	_____

Gauge   Other Tools

_____ sts per _____ inch(es)   _____

_____ rows per _____ inch(es)   _____

Knitting Journal

Project: _____

Start Date: _____ Finish: _____

Measurements: _____

Materials	Quantity
_____	_____
_____	_____
_____	_____

Needles	Embellishments
_____	_____
_____	_____

Gauge	Other Tools
_____ sts per _____ inch(es)	_____
_____ rows per _____ inch(es)	_____

Knitting Journal

Project: _____

Start Date: _____ Finish: _____

Measurements: _____

Materials	Quantity
_____	_____
_____	_____
_____	_____

Needles	Embellishments
_____	_____
_____	_____

Gauge   Other Tools

_____ sts per _____ inch(es)   _____

_____ rows per _____ inch(es)   _____

Knitting Journal

Project: _____

Start Date: _____ Finish: _____

Measurements: _____

Materials	Quantity
_____	_____
_____	_____
_____	_____

Needles	Embellishments
_____	_____
_____	_____

Gauge	Other Tools
_____ sts per _____ inch(es)	_____
_____ rows per _____ inch(es)	_____

Knitting Journal

Project: _____

Start Date: _____ Finish: _____

Measurements: _____

Materials   Quantity

_____   _____

_____   _____

_____   _____

Needles   Embellishments

_____   _____

_____   _____

Gauge   Other Tools

____sts per ____ inch(es)   _____

____rows per ____ inch(es)   _____

Knitting Journal

Project: _____

Start Date: _____ Finish: _____

Measurements: _____

Materials	Quantity
_____	_____
_____	_____
_____	_____

Needles	Embellishments
_____	_____
_____	_____

Gauge	Other Tools
_____ sts per _____ inch(es)	_____
_____ rows per _____ inch(es)	_____

Knitting Journal

Project: _____

Start Date: _____ Finish: _____

Measurements: _____

Materials	Quantity
_____	_____
_____	_____
_____	_____

Needles	Embellishments
_____	_____
_____	_____

Gauge	Other Tools
____sts per ____ inch(es)	_____
____rows per ____ inch(es)	_____

Knitting Journal

Project: _____

Start Date: _____ Finish: _____

Measurements: _____

Materials   Quantity

_____   _____

_____   _____

_____   _____

Needles   Embellishments

_____   _____

_____   _____

Gauge   Other Tools

_____sts per _____ inch(es)   _____

_____rows per _____ inch(es)   _____

Knitting Journal

Project: _____

Start Date:_____ Finish: _____

Measurements: _____

Materials   Quantity

_____   _____

_____   _____

_____   _____

Needles   Embellishments

_____   _____

_____   _____

Gauge   Other Tools

_____sts per _____ inch(es)   _____

_____rows per _____ inch(es)   _____

Knitting Journal

Project: _____

Start Date: _____ Finish: _____

Measurements: _____

Materials	Quantity
_____	_____
_____	_____
_____	_____

Needles	Embellishments
_____	_____
_____	_____

Gauge	Other Tools
____ sts per ____ inch(es)	_____
____ rows per ____ inch(es)	_____

Knitting Journal

Project: _____

Start Date: _____ Finish: _____

Measurements: _____

Materials	Quantity
_____	_____
_____	_____
_____	_____

Needles	Embellishments
_____	_____
_____	_____

Gauge	Other Tools
_____ sts per _____ inch(es)	_____
_____ rows per _____ inch(es)	_____

Made in the USA
Monee, IL
06 October 2020